(5) 160775 4

D0030812

ALSO BY DAVID MURA

Poetry
After We Lost Our Way (1989)

Nonfiction
A Male Grief: Notes on Pornography and Addiction (1987)
Turning Japanese: Memoirs of a Sansei (1991)

THE
COLORS
OF DESIRE

PIERCE COLLEGE LIBRARY
PUYALLUP WA 98374
LAKEWOOD WA 98498

THE
COLORS
OF DESIRE

POEMS

DAVID MURA

ANCHOR BOOKS

NEW YORK · LONDON · TORONTO · SYDNEY · AUCKLAND

AN ANCHOR BOOK

PUBLISHED BY DOUBLEDAY

a division of Bantam Doubleday Dell Publishing Group, Inc.

1540 Broadway, New York, New York 10036

ANCHOR BOOKS, DOUBLEDAY, and the portrayal of an anchor

are trademarks of Doubleday, a division of Bantam Doubleday

Dell Publishing Group, Inc.

Book design by Julie Duquet

Library of Congress Cataloging-in-Publication Data

Mura, David.

The colors of desire : poems / David Mura.

p.   cm.

I. Title.

PS3563.U68C65   1995

811'.54—dc20   95-6587

CIP

ISBN 0-385-47460-1 (hardcover)

ISBN 0-385-47461-X (paperback)

Copyright © 1995 by David Mura

ALL RIGHTS RESERVED

PRINTED IN THE UNITED STATES OF AMERICA

FIRST ANCHOR BOOKS EDITION: January 1995

1   3   5   7   9   10   8   6   4   2

ACKNOWLEDGMENTS

The poems in this volume were previously published in the following publications:

Asian America: "Harvest at Minidoka Internment Camp"
Crazyhorse: "Listening," "To H.N."
Colorado Review: "The Colors of Desire"
Indiana Review: "Notes on Pornography Abandoned," "Issei: Song of the First Years in America"
The New England Review: "The Blueness of the Day"
Green Mountains Review: "Gardens We Have Left"
The River Styx: "Issei Strawberry"

"Listening" reprinted in *The Best of Crazyhorse* and *The 1990 Puschart Prize XV (1990–1991).* The poem was printed as a special chapbook, *Listening,* published by the Minnesota Center for Book Arts, illustrated and designed by Kinji Akagawa.

"The Colors of Desire" won first place in the 1991 Martha Scott Trimble Poetry Award given by *The Colorado Review* and was reprinted in *New American Poets of the '90's* (Godine Press, 1991).

"Gardens We Have Left" was also published in *The Open Boat: Poems from Asian America* (Anchor/Doubleday, 1993).

"To H.N." and "Chorus on the Origins of Lust" are included in *Premonitions: The Kaya Anthology of New Asian American Poetry* (Kaya, 1994).

My gratitude to Cyrus Cassells, Charles Flowers, Garrett Hongo, Deborah Keenan, Susan Mitchell, David Wojahn, and especially to my *hakujin no tomodachi* for their generous help on this manuscript. The late Lynda Hull, a remarkable poet, was a valuable teacher and critic for me. My thanks also to Li-Young Lee, Valerie Lee, Sheila Murphy, Alexs Pate, Gerald Stern, Quincy Troupe, and Alan Soldofsky for their support. This work was supported by funds from the National Endowment for the Arts, the Bush Foundation, the Loft McKnight Award of Distinction, the Minnesota State Arts Board, and the Rockefeller Foundation's Bellagio Retreat Center. Finally, my greatest debt and thanks and love go to my wife, Susie, without whom these pages would not exist.

For Aunt Ruth, Aunt Baye, and Aunt Miwako

CONTENTS

1

2

3

4

THE
COLORS
OF DESIRE

1

ISSEI STRAWBERRY

Taste this strawberry, spin it in motion
on the whirl of your tongue, look west
towards Watsonville or some other
sleepy California town, spit
and wipe your sleeve across
your mouth, then bend down again, dipping
and rising like a piston, like fire, like a swirling
dervish, a lover ready to ravish this harvest, this
autumn of thirty-one or eight or nine, years
when, as everyone declines
around you, as swing and Capra redefine
an American dream, as some are deferred and some
preferred, and some complain, and some confer
and strike, and are stricken, are written
out of history, you have managed your own
prosperity, a smacking ripeness on the vine, acres
and acres you mine as your own, as your children's
whose deed it is, knowing you own nothing
here, you're no one here
but your genes, the ones who spit back
so readily English on their tongues, tart
and trickier, phrases that blow past
you, winking, even as they
sink in, you're losing
them, you're gaining a harvest, a country, a future,
so much to lose when, in biting your tongue,
the red juice flows between your teeth
with the memory of strawberries
and loam and sweat, of summers in the valley
when you made it before the war had come.

THE COLORS OF DESIRE

1 *Photograph of a Lynching (circa 1930)*

These men? In their dented felt hats,
in the way their fingers tug their suspenders or vests,
with faces a bit puffy or too lean, eyes narrow and close together,
they seem too like our image of the South,
the Thirties. Of course they are white;
who then could create this cardboard figure, face
flat and grey, eyes oversized, bulging like
an ancient totem this gang has dug up? At the far right,
in a small browed cap, a boy of twelve smiles,
as if responding to what's most familiar here:
the camera's click. And though directly above them,
a branch ropes the dead negro in the air,
the men too focus their blank beam
on the unseen eye. Which is, at this moment, us.

Or, more precisely, me. Who cannot but recall
how my father, as a teenager, clutched his weekend pass,
passed through the rifle towers and gates
of the Jerome, Arkansas, camp, and, in 1942,
stepped on a bus to find white riders
motioning, "Sit here, son," and, in the rows beyond,
a half dozen black faces, waving him back,
"Us colored folks got to stick together."
How did he know where to sit? And how is it,

thirty-five years later, I found myself sitting
in a dark theater, watching *Behind the Green Door*
with a dozen anonymous men? On the screen
a woman sprawls on a table, stripped, the same one

on the Ivory Snow soap box, a baby on her shoulder,
smiling her blond, practically pure white smile.
Now, after being prepared and serviced slowly
by a handful of women, as one of them
kneels, buries her face in her crotch,
she is ready: And now he walks in—

Lean, naked, black, streaks of white paint on his chest
and face, a necklace of teeth, it's almost comical,
this fake garb of the jungle, Africa and All-America,
black and blond, almost a joke but for the surge
of what these lynchers urged as the ultimate crime
against nature: the black man kneeling to this kidnapped
body, slipping himself in, the screen showing it all, down
to her head shaking in a seizure, the final scream
before he lifts himself off her quivering body . . .

I left that theater, bolted from a dream into a dream.
I stared at the cars whizzing by, watched the light change,
red, yellow, green, and the haze in my head from the hash,
and the haze in my head from the image, melded together,
                    reverberating.
I don't know what I did afterwards. Only, night after night,
I will see those bodies, black and white (and where am I,
the missing third?), like a talisman, a rageful, unrelenting release.

2 *1957*

Cut to Chicago, June. A boy of six.
Next year my hero will be Mickey Mantle,
but this noon, as father eases the Bel-Air past Wilson,
with cowboy hat black, cocked at an angle,
my skin dark from the sun, I'm Paladin,
and my six-guns point at cars whizzing past,

blast after blast ricocheting the glass.
Like all boys in such moments, my face
attempts a look of what—toughness? bravado? ease?—
until, impatient, my father's arm wails
across the seat, and I sit back, silent at last.

Later, as we step from IGA with our sacks,
a man in a serge suit—stained with ink?—
steps forward, shouts, "Hey, you a Jap?
You from Tokyo? You a Jap? A Chink?"
I stop, look up, I don't know him,
my arm yanks forward, and suddenly,
the sidewalk's rolling, buckling, like lava melting,
and I know father will explode,
shouts, fists, I know his temper.
And then,
I'm in that dream where nothing happens—
The ignition grinds, the man's face presses
the windshield, and father stares ahead,
fingers rigid on the wheel . . .

That night in my bedroom, moths,
like fingertips, peck the screen;
from the living room, the muffled t.v.
As I imagine Shane stepping into the dusty street,
in the next bed, my younger brother starts
to taunt—*you can't hurt me, you can't hurt me* . . .
Who can explain where this chant began?
Or why, when father throws the door open,
shouts stalking chaos erupted in his house,
he swoops on his son with the same swift motion
that the son, like an animal, like a scared and angry little boy,
fell on his brother, beating him in the dark?

3 *Miss June 1964*

I'm twelve, home from school
with a slight fever. I slide back the door
of my parents' closet—my mother's out shopping—
rummage among pumps, flats, lined in a rack,
unzip the garment bags, one by one.
It slides like a sigh from the folded sweaters.
I flip through ads for cologne, L.P.'s, a man
in a trench coat, lugging a panda-sized Fleischman's fifth.
Somewhere past the photo of Schweitzer
in his pith helmet, and the cartoon nude man
perched as a gargoyle, I spill the photo
millions of men, white, black, yellow, have seen,
though the body before me is white, eighteen:
Her breasts are enormous, almost frightening
—the areolas seem large as my fist.
As the three glossy pages sprawl before me,
I start to touch myself, and there is
some terror, my mother will come home,
some delight I've never felt before,
and I do not cry out, I make no sound . . .

How did I know that photo was there?
Or mother know I knew?
Two nights later, at her request,
father lectures me on burning out too early.
Beneath the cone of light at the kitchen table,
we're caught, like the shiest of lovers.
He points at the booklet from the AMA
—he writes their P.R.—"Read it," he says,
"and, if you have any questions . . ."

Thirty years later, these questions remain.
And his answers, too, are still the same:
Really, David, it was just a magazine.
And the camps, my father's lost nursery,
the way he chased me round the yard in L.A.,
even the two by four he swung—why connect them
with years you wandered those theaters?
Is nothing in your life your own volition?
The past isn't just a box full of horrors.
What of those mornings in the surf
near Venice, all of us casting line after line,
arcing over breakers all the way from Japan,
or plopping down beside my mother,
a plateful of mochi, *pulling it like taffy*
with our teeth, shoyu *dribbling*
down our chins. Think of it, David.
There were days like that. We were happy. . . .

4

Who hears the rain churning the forest to mud,
or the unraveling rope snap, the negro
plummet to rest at last? And what flooded my father's eyes
in the Little Rock theater, sitting beneath the balcony
in that third year of war? Where is 1944,
its snows sweeping down Heart Mountain,
to vanish on my mother's black bobbing head,
as she scurries towards the cramped cracked barracks
where her mother's throat coughs through the night,
and her father sits beside her on the bed?
The dim bulb flickers as my mother enters.
Her face is flushed, her cheeks cold. She
bows, unwraps her scarf, pours the steaming

kettle in the tea pot; offers her mother a sip.
And none of them knows she will never
talk of this moment, that, years later,
I will have to imagine it, again and again,
just as I have tried to imagine the lives
of all those who have entered these lines . . .

Tonight snow drifts below my window,
and lamps puff ghostly aureoles
over walks and lawns. Father, mother,
I married a woman not of my color.
What is it I want to escape?
These nights in our bed, my head
on her belly, I can hear these thumps,
and later, when she falls asleep,
I stand in our daughter's room,
so bare yet but for a simple wooden crib
(on the bulletin board I've pinned the sonogram
with black and white swirls like a galaxy
spinning about the fetal body),
and something plummets inside me,
out of proportion to the time
I've been portioned on this earth.
And if what is granted erases nothing,
if history remains, untouched, implacable,
as darkness flows up our hemisphere,
her hollow still moves moonward,
small hill on the horizon, swelling,
floating with child, white, yellow,
who knows, who can tell her,

oh why must it matter?

CHORUS ON THE ORIGINS OF HIS LUST

Come, come, we've heard this before.
You think, in this age, anyone cares?
What we really can't forgive is a bore.

You seem to believe in sin
as if you'd been dunked as a boy
in some red-clay river and born again.

This is merely the excellent sophistry
of the age: that, in our sickness,
we can make of our guilt a family,

and instead of the proprietary
influence of stars, Orion
and the Dog snarling overhead,

or the Scorpion raising its tail
on our birth or bridal bed,
we say each disaster that assails

comes simply from the primal
Oedipal, Electric scene:
Father, mother, child in hell.

Or take this second dispensation:
That in the firmament rising
above a boy's masturbation,

the planetary dream of a world
whitened, nightmares of
yellow, dark-skinned hordes,

all fissioned desire, as if nothing
in his nature grew naturally
perverted, lecherous, wild. Your

goatish glint, where did it twinkle?
In the eye of mother? Father?
Or guards in the towers

at Minidoka, Jerome? Nonsense.
Cock, bull, you made these disasters . . .
—Yes, yes, I acknowledge my own.

NOTES ON PORNOGRAPHY ABANDONED

1

Yesterday, past the oak, the wicker chairs,
friends kept knocking wooden balls; shouts,
laughter, echoing on the lawn. On the tape player
a cello concerto ballooned upwards to
an endless blue. Watching I felt like some count
in Chekhov, wry, foolish, Russian. Later,
picking up the plates, like tiny moons gathered
in her grasp, my wife floated through the dark,
beautiful, ghostly in gauze white pleats.
A shudder swept through me, half guilt, half fear,
nothing I could quite name: just a chill,
as if nothing had changed . . .

2

Always there's this memory cut open like a fig, bursting with seeds.
There's the late spring when the sheets like a flock of doves
scatter and rush with the wind on the lines. There's
an apartment complex across the alley, moths
battering the screen with tiny wings, and I, sixteen,
look up from the *Genealogy:*
Of course, I see it, her window. She pulls the pins
from her hair, pulls off her uniform,
and there's a falling, a slicing of the cord
so some cry can break free, and her bra slides
off like the slow tilting of snow, sliding to an avalanche,
just above the valley where desire sleeps. Rooted tight,
I stare and stare,
and even when her lights go off, when I start to tell myself—

go to sleep, forget it, you'll never do this again . . .—it
dropped like a plummet in my conscience:

No, no, no, no. You cannot stop . . .

3

It was in the bookstore, another endless session:
Settled in a booth, putting in quarter after quarter
for film, I turned, saw an eye peering through
this hole cut in the wall, and then,
like a flag of surrender, a penis: ridiculous, pathetic,
hard. As the woman on the screen shouted, coming
again and again, pounding the bed, her face
twisted like an astronaut pulled by G's,
I felt this rush, this fix at the center.
And found myself kneeling, unable to stop . . .
Then a warm saltiness spread on my tongue; slipping
off the shaft, soft, sticky as taffy, I knew I'd
crossed one more line. And nothing, nothing happened . . .

4

What gain does the pimp, the devourer of pornography,
seek through the nerves, the depositions and debits,

the checks of the brain? He fills an emptiness in himself
through creating emptiness elsewhere. But where is

that elsewhere? In his empathy, his wish to see others
suffer exactly what he suffers, he finds a face, a body,

a blank moan; a woman who must remain mute so his
pleasure can exist. And in that muteness his pleasure, his power, hides . . .

5

Four years ago today, believing
The "I" who I was has been leveled as by a great wind,

I poured them in the dumpster, the glossy pages unfolding, spilling
like liquid dreams. Doused them with gas.

A mother called in the dark, *Jimmy, Jimmy Lee* . . . The match
          popped.
And faces, naked bodies, flamed, curled

to ash, smoke sifting through my lungs, blood, brain.
And something caved inside me, some long, slow, unrepentant sigh.

I thought of how, during the war, the Vietnamese communists
took the southern prostitutes to a camp

where all day they would play games, sing songs, run races,
eat and sleep like children, exactly like children.

I'd read—but didn't quite believe—that some, some did recover . . .

ISSEI: SONG OF THE FIRST YEARS IN AMERICA

Our hair in chignons, we crowd down the planks,
our legs still wobbly from weeks at sea.
I do not expect him to be
handsome as the photo
but this is not even the same man.
The wind blows salt spray in my eyes.
Behind me I hear Keiko's muffled sobs,
the awkward greetings of a couple
who will spend half a century together.
I stare at his face. I bow.
That night it is over so quickly,
for days after, when I walk,
I feel this pebble in my shoe.
He says I must stop
eating like a sumo, must give him
a son, must clean, cook, sew—No, I think,
that is the other man, the snake that vanished
in the river in my dream, the owl
who hoots each night in the grove beyond
the rows of tomatoes and beans.
As crickets skim their cries across the night,
I squeeze a scarf between my teeth, slide
my hands open like the branches of a cedar.
Who is it who hacks here? Is this
what a baby hears inside, a howling,
a throbbing almost like love?

I hear a crow squawk overhead,
and the night darkens.

We are far from the city,
and the seasons do not change.
The air is dry as rice powder.
We live in a house where I can see a star
or two in the corner of the roof.
He is a man whose dreams have been stolen,
who lumbers about, picks me up
the way a bear would handle
a *raku* bowl. He curses the dry heat, *hakujin,*
my laziness and appetite. But I am not
a courtesan. I am a peasant's daughter.
One day, after years in the fields,
my spine will crumple like *obaa-san.*
Each night I taste the sweat from his face
as it streams down and he thrashes at my thighs.
There are no ghosts here, no Buddha,
no *torrii.* We sometimes eat oranges.
We have a bath. I am thankful for that.

It is noon, heat floods the fields in waves.
The tomatoes cave in, like the faces
of old drunks. He shoves away
the emptied bowl of rice, the grains
like tiny insect eggs. I tell myself
I am dark, delicate as ashes. As he
walks through me to the door, I leave
smudges on his soles. Something warm
billows between my legs. Pain like a plow
cleaves through me. He's back at the door,
his face whiter than my teeth. Is that
my voice calling? I hear drops plop

on the boards. Behind me
a snake coils and hisses, another
dark woman is stirring the broth.
The stove flames, an infant wails,
cicadas hum in the eucalyptus.
And like the sun splitting up the rim
of the world, in that sea behind me
when Japan fell from sight, everything
swims with redness, a blood soaked light.

It was a girl. Who passed more quickly
than a fever, firefly, haiku. A whippoorwill
flutes through the blue night. He
will buy a few more acres next spring, he says,
he will hire a Filipino, will plant
an orange grove. Each night
he's gone, it gets easier,
like the days of summer. Each night
he finds in the cards some luck
both of us own. Eyes like burnt almonds,
gaze like a blackbird's—He sees
how empty I am, how much I can't give up.
I watch him nudge his team down the road.
The first fat shoots throb up from the fields,
a rabbit scurries between cabbages. Chickens
squawk in their cages. *Aka-chan,* little ghost,
eat up every part of me. Make me disappear . . .

2

TO H.N.

It is always easy to sentimentalize old lovers. They are distant
and distance, we have heard, increases desire.
You live now a few miles down the freeway, and years ago.
How I wish there were rice fields, an ocean, between us,
a hedge of fox gloves, rows of sweet peas, cedar forests, canyons,
         deserts,
and a story of plane wheels screeching on the tarmac
or helicopters lifting above a city, tiny figures, stick-like, like those a
         child draws,
hanging from the landing rim, falling to the sea.
It would have been history then, not me, who failed you.
My guilt would be greater and therefore, more easy.

I recall your father, who still sews in a store I sometimes pass.
And your mother who served me steaming bowls, riddled with
         coriander, globes of oil,
a pepper that stung my eyes to tears. And your sisters, each younger,
more fluent than you. And one, more beautiful. (In those days
there was little I refused.) And your brothers who, with sticks on
         strings,
fought on the streets, in school corridors, the shouts of chink and
         gook,
claiming a fierceness that surprised their larger white opponents.
Twelve of you in a three-bedroom flat. I sat at the table
and read with you through Fitzgerald, O'Connor's story of the Bible
         salesman
who steals the crippled girl's wooden leg, leaves her stranded in the
         hayloft
in a cracker Georgia. You were eighteen. Your mother thought
I was teaching you English. Seeing in your family my father's
a half century before, I almost believed that. Sometimes

we went roller-skating, to a movie, disobeying your parents.
I went home afterwards to the woman I was living with. Who
        became my wife.

What else? You'd lived in Vientiane, spoke Laotian, Vietnamese.
I recall moments in a car, on my couch, in my bed.
And still can't stop. Won't make amends.
A cousin of yours was among the bones they dug up
in Hue. You got used to our winters, their icy winds.
I flunked out of grad school. You graduated one May.

And what it all adds up to I can't tell.
An accident of history? Something sordid, brief, betrayed?
You were beautiful. The only Asian woman I've ever touched,
        reaching
beyond the mirror of my own self-hatred, propelled by my lust.
And there was this night, at the top of the tallest building in town,
looking down at the lights and car beams shuttling towards the
        horizon,
when you bent by a candle-flame, said you would never forget this
        night.

But somehow I suspect that for you, as for me, that memory now
        means little.
You're probably indifferent. Which is just as well.

THE BLUENESS OF THE DAY

1 Mizuno in Paris (1947)

It happened in an instant:

On the ridge, shells gutted up dirt and smoke,
a hundred mouths gaping at once . . . In that streaming,

through leafless woods rinsed with light,

thirty yards ahead, Shig aimed;
at this high whine, palpable as a spear

drilled through my eardrum, I hurled my weight to

earth. I still see my body arched like that, leaping,
as if I were somehow there

and not there, freed from myself . . .

I envied Shig. Whenever he entered a church,
in Rome, Naples, Paris, something
spoke to him, not about the strangeness

of living on earth, but some magical
promise, whatever it is
a clever boy sees in a broken toy.

In camp, our families were stuck
in the same barracks, separated by sheets:
snores, arguments, night noises of

our parents, war clips on the radio flooded
our dreams. That day we signed up with
the guards in the towers, we held the flag

to our hearts, staring in disbelief and wonder.
Shig was smiling, the stupid fuck.
But then, so was I, so was I . . .

It was all so predictable, so mechanical:
Like the way mother would raise her
cleaver, crunch its blade through the chicken's

joints, searing the limbs. Or the way,
seconds earlier, she drained its neck
in the dirt, thumbing blood from

the spongy windpipe, squeezing out its
wheezy squawk. It's like that German boy,
he was a boy, really, his straw colored hair,

ruddy translucent skin, the way he stared
at me, my bayonet in his belly, at me,
as if he'd suddenly discovered his one true

connection to the world. I can see his face
when I close my eyes, smell the rain flashing near
the Arno, thunder that seemed to shake

the fields of green wet wheat, like
girls tossing salt spray from their hair.
—Yes, I never felt more alive . . .

"Okaa-san, life is glorious here. Death
too. In the mirror I see the lines of bewilderment

that creased your face

as *otoo-san* stumbled each night
in the barracks, mumbling *sakura, sakura . . .*

Sometimes I think of what my hands have done,

what my eyes have seen,
and none of it connects to that face, staring back at me,

its smooth dark skin: I am sick of being

decent, dependable, Japanese . . ."
—Each night I write this letter;

each night it comes back: *Sender Unknown.*

Once I worked with my father
in the orange groves. Frost
was coming that night,
and we set out smudge pots, smoke
rising amid the wet leaves.
We were too hurried to speak, lighting

and laying them down, row on row.
I recall the black chortles of the crickets,
the bull frog in the ditch,
and the light at the tip of my father's cigar,
bobbing in the dark. The frost
never came, the oranges were saved,
hanging there, heavy
and round as breasts
the day we moved out, the early
light lifting mist from the fields,
their green shade. Mother carried our lunch
in a *furoshiki,* Ginny her doll,
and the smell of *shoyu* was still
in the hall as I walked out the door.
I remember we said nothing, knew
nothing could be said. We
left the brass Buddha in the basement.
Who could we sell it to?
When father stepped towards the car,
he stepped across the morning
sun, and his body turned
to light, and I knew I hated him, his sharp
commands, *"Hayaku, hayaku . . ."*
his useless tongue. And then,

then the gates opened.

Shig's letter scatters on the floor. It started
with a story I'd heard before: How, when he set off,
his father took him by the shoulders

—he paid no attention to the guards at the gate—
"This is your country. Make me proud."
(Mine spat at me: "Bakka, when they let me out, then

I'll sign the oath.") Well, Shig did come home, only
one arm was gone, and after they'd feasted
on *tempura* and *sake,* after they'd laughed themselves drunk,

the father took Shig to the *ofuro,* helped him in,
and began, slowly, gently, lathering the stump,
the back where black peppers of shrapnel worked themselves

out like points of a pencil. All the while
he sang a Japanese lullaby, one
Shig recalled from childhood . . .

—What is it I can't believe?
In the prairie grass, on the hill outside
of camp, we buried a few Issei

and a baby, flung like a seed
in the maw of earth. Last night
I saw my mother there, laying out

plates of *teriyaki, gohan, mochi.*
She arranged four sets of *hashi,*
and I thought it was for our family,

but when she turned and looked
back at me, I knew: It was
oshoshiki. Food for the dead . . .

❦

"Okaa-san, you ask me why I will not come home:
But we only explain suffering to console

ourselves . . . It is chance, not God

or *Dharma,* which placed me here, wounded,
surviving, possessing nothing. *Okaa-san,*

there were camps here

so much more hideous than ours:
Our suffering so small it might have seemed

paradise to these. *Okaa-san,*

even in my worst rages
I could not slash the Mona Lisa or the sinners of Caravaggio—

What allowed me to do what I have done? . . .

Okaa-san, think of this space between us
as the wall where messages

are scraped out between two prisoners . . ."

—The words vanish.
I begin again. . . .

❦

I walk the streets to keep awake.
The empty parks, pigeons, strollers, gutters
streaming with rain. Patisseries, flower stalls,

gendarmes, bicycles, boucheries. Stones
in the cemeteries with legendary names.
Bridges, grey and rain-beaten, arched

above the Seine. Poles marking an angle
on the banks. Is it better to say, "I am suffering,"
than "This landscape is ugly"? Each evening

an alarm goes off. I start walking again.
When I see them beneath a street light,
or lounging in doors, their perfume

already trudging up a stairway to this small room,
I know I am so far past bitterness
I must be bitterness itself.

Near morning, in a tiny room in Pigalle,
I'll rise, dress, the smell of her submission
on my cheeks, a pile of cigarettes

left by the bed. And for a few minutes, I'll keep
her face beneath me, almost dead, almost
frightened of whatever she sees there:

I've thought so often it's my skin, the folds
of my eyes, the alien energy thrashing her thighs,
but no, it's just my face, that implacable mask . . .

2 Intermission (1991)

This is a draft in progress. As in a film without stars:

And the camera circles
                 the face of a Japanese-
American, cigarette tilted off his lip,
                       smoke curling from the tip.
Cut to his eyes, the cobbles on the street,
                     the balconies,
their eight feet windows
                 and black metal frames,
and the gutters swirling
                 with an evening's rain.
(Of course, I'd prefer black and white, the colors
                   of Resnais,
Hiroshima Mon Amour.)
                 Cut back to scenes
of the lovers in bed, the crenellations
                 of flesh,
vines scrawling up a building,
                 a stocking laced like a question
mark on the crumpled sheets.
                 Her back arches above him,
we see her torso, the ribs
                 like grillwork, the nipples
taut, the aureole
               just off center, so that the streetlight
flashes on sweat beads,
                 and beyond a blueness
only filming at night
               can achieve. Her mouth whimpers, moans,
and we cut

to a cone of light above a desk, her hands
on a typewriter
       the keys pattering out the letters
of a novel, two lovers
           in bed—A room with shutters,
shouts from the streets, charcoal fires,
              Chinese soups,
a fan above the bed,
      whirling—Cut
        from the words
to her cigarette in the ash tray,
        the remains of a pack
stubbed out, traces of lipstick
        at the still moist tips.

It's too romantic. Tear it up. Start again.

The interviewer in my living room pokes and prods:
"There's a brutality in your work," she says, "you use
the word white man the way an existentialist uses God . . ."

Taking the cue—Oh yes, the angry artist of color—
I start spouting Marxist ditties. Cut to reaction shots
of her chin nodding, then quizzical, wondering

what the hell Marxism means to anyone, now the wall
has collapsed. I drone on . . . This isn't Malibu, of course.
It's cozy St. Paul. My *happa* daughter shouts down the hall.

"Perhaps the author might better publish his material
in *Penthouse* . . ." The flip-side too plays just as well:

"This knee-jerk feminist charade . . ." Or: "Where is the
       lyrical? . . .

There is simply no strong, personal presence. . . ."
Well, why tryst a Nisei with a Pigalle whore
who turns out to be a member of the resistance

very like, no, who is, Marguerite Duras?
And why flesh this out on screen? *Always there*
and elsewhere at once—I cough, her pen pauses—

the actors possess the multiple presence of deities.
(Can we choose the bodies that fill our dreams?)
"Got to have a yellow woman"—yes I know that ditty—

"if you're a yellow man . . ." Why give a shit
about the 442nd? *The face in the mirror: It doesn't fit.*

❦

As in a film:
    Silence. The lighthouse spinning
                    its shadows through the room:
"It was in Cholon . . ." *she says.*
        Or: ". . . in Calcutta . . ."
                    Or: ". . . in Nevers . . ."
(I think of the German artist
            I met in Tokyo,
                    her father who made films in Berlin
during the war, the skeletons
            in charcoal of her early work, soft
                    and ashen, lyrically grotesque.)
Cut to his face,
            to a flash of a twig, snow melting
                    in droplets, the concave curled vision they
                                    give.
Boots, mud crusted laces.
            A green fatigued leg.
                    Hands flat against the belly.
Which, as the camera moves farther,
            brings a small trickle of red,
                    like a stray thread, clinging
to his knuckles.
            His face (serene or twisted: shoot both,
                    later in the cutting room, see).
Cut to
            her face, against the bedboard,
                    she's clutching her knees, the sheet
flowing as he moves himself up
            on his elbow, still listening. The lighthouse

flashes on his face. The screen goes

black . . .

Yes, as in a film: *Fields of wild mustard, a river*

empties into the sea,

a white sand beach, gulls in V's.

In the room, she plays

Piaf over and over. Shadows

like lizards flit

across their bodies. Her thighs

shiny, slippery as melons.

His chin darker with stubble.

Cut to dialogue mocking the dour

concierge, their faces in laughter louder,

raucous, flashes of teeth, hysterical,

obscene . . .

3 Sentences by M. Duras (dates unknown)

"The Nisei? He went as he came, without hesitation, without warning. Still, I'm sure there was a time he asked: Should I go back to her? It could have been me, or his mother, or another whore. A girl of his kind. Near the end we would weep, gushing sobs. As if we'd been drinking. It didn't matter if we were touching or across the room, staring. And we were happy as never before . . .

"Wherever I go it's disappearing. Bistros, movies about the war, death. Carrying a kind of nostalgia about himself, when he entered the café, in the state he was in, I wanted to die too, in the same theatrical manner. He asked if I was used to death. No, those were never the specific words, those are lost, unusable . . .

"In the unity of the book something always explodes. It's like writing a scene—A quay: the Mekong River. Black junks moored to the banks. Young musicians, mandolins. Soup vendors with pots simmering over fires on the decks. Singing. I told him of the beggar woman, who walked the shore, steps heavy like a peasant. How I caught this snake gliding through the shallows, lanterns shimmering on the tar black waters. The smell was unforgettable. He stroked my legs. It reminded me of him. We left Paris, rented a room near the Mediterranean. Years later, in India, the beggar woman came back. Destroy, she said . . .

"Once I mentioned the camps, Robert L., my first husband. The American soldiers, mostly blacks, wore gas masks against typhus, the fear was so great. He said, 'I dreamed of killing all the people I've ever lived with,' including his boyhood friend, the German soldier in the woods, his first lover, me. He dreamed it several times about each of us. They snuck Robert out, disguised his skeletal remains in two uniforms as a French officer. Held him as he walked. If they'd suspected his state, they'd have left him with the dying . . . All this will happen naturally, of course. And then, for a very long time.

"In every war movie, there's a secret adoration of war. It's the same with your poem, even as you call 'into question.' Sooner or later, you're bound to do it in real life. His hands grew rough on my body. The pleasure was mortal. I write: 'Home, in the north, where children play . . . Home, where she is going, to be beaten by her mother, to be beaten to death.' I know so little about Americans, though I know he was and was not like them. I asked him inside. He gave me cigarettes. Though we never spoke of it, not that first night, nor any time after, I think he thought I was his whore. Oh yes, he knew I wrote. That I would write about him . . .

"One evening the wind dropped, riders on horses pounded the surf. Then the doors were banging. Shouts. It was them, them back from Germany. I had this sensation always that he was coming back. I prefer men who walk, one after the other, who go there for a reason as inevitable as fate. And it's true, the hole makes people sick. Even men. Everyone says, 'Yes, yes, Marguerite Duras,' but read the books. There's no one there. The riders have nothing to do with the walkers."

4 *Marguerite (Pigalle, the Mediterranean, 1947)*

I thought your body would be soft like a woman's.
Your cheekbones are so rounded, your eyes curled
like sleep. You still wear the uniform. Why?

I had a lover once like you. In that city where
the Mekong dragged down half a continent, boats,
water buffaloes, crates, chairs, tigers, palm trees,

I was crossing on the ferry to school one morning,
and out of a black limousine stepped a Chinese,
in a white tussore suit, the suit of a banker . . . It seems

so long ago, those continents, those cities: Calcutta,
Phnom Penh, Rome, Bonn, Marseilles, Algiers.
And each with its lover. Even then the Chinese

said I would love love. . . . But you're not like him.
There's this scar across your belly. Another on your lip.
Your French is like a child's. We speak in English.

On the ferry, I was wearing a man's fedora,
gold lamé shoes, a white dress cinched at the waist
by my brother's belt. I looked like a child prostitute.

Perhaps that's what you mistook tonight in me.
You rise to the window, light a cigarette.
When you turn, my face is covered with black

sheer silk, my tongue thrust forward, blue flames
of light brim in the mirror over the roofs of Paris,
a pigeon like a bullet sails out of sight, and you

fall upon me, diving through the surface, lungs bursting,
you can't see, can't hear, and still your flesh beats
against me like the sea. You don't come up.

❧

I can see a lighthouse at the end of the jetty.
Waves crash there, spill with sunlight on the floor.
Our towels billow on the terrace. A week

has passed. (They say even the continents are shifting
—a little south, a little east.) I walk across a room,
you finger my nipple. Pull me towards you . . .

You know I'm not the girl from Bruyeres. The one
who sliced bread for you. Her father sang drinking songs.
Her brother eyed you like a Vichy collaborator.

"We came down the hills, and the villagers edged
forward, carrying baskets. When they saw our faces,
they looked puzzled—Japonais? Comment? . . ." *(How*

she slipped like water from the fist of your mind.)
You don't want me to speak. I nod. Exhaustion's
a shape I'm used to. My limbs are so thin, wiry

as a farmboy's. So conscious of their whiteness,
tufts of hair in my underarms, sliding into me like
lightning without thunder—flash, darkness, silence—

you lift my body, stagger with me to the terrace,
and if, one day, all this will return to me
etched in black on the blankness of a page,

as wind, sand, salt and sun, lather our flesh
to a froth, nothing cries out, nothing gives way—
what vanishes is the sea, the blueness of day.

A gull wedges its white in the sky. The sand,
bleached to a fine, grainy white, sticks to your skin.
I scrape you against my flesh like a pumice stone.

There are little stones on the beach, the shells
like eyelids, pink and azure; tan, vermillion.
We are, I suppose, flowing into each other,

getting lost, the way lovers do, and so
don't know each other, but enter to find
these rooms unavailable, cluttered with furniture

someone sat in, like the house in the woods
with the porridge still hot, steaming
and no one home, no one to remember

the beds we slept in, sheets portraying the wrinkles
that scald our faces, years from now. I am already
forgetting your name. Or the letter that arrived

saying you have to return, it is too late,
your mother is dead. Clairvoyance failed you.
And my skin glowing in the dark, milky

as the eyes of someone whose sight has
been shattered since birth. You tell me
the earth is filthy and throwing us in her arms?

What will you say you found there? It's growing
colder. I can smell the iodine in the air. A
rankness of seaweeds. Our bodies. Where? Where?

Years later you'll return to Paris,
the cobblestone streets, cafés, lamps,
gutters where rainwater flows with all
the resonance a mirror lacks. You'll recall

how useless you felt, how that city
was like finding in a forest the honey
of wild bees. A stage with backdrops
more brilliant, more authorial, than life.

Of course, the streets of Pigalle
where women step from shadows
beneath neon are still there. Cold,
and living like a branch in March.

And you, you're a businessman, your company
intact, your time free. As through the wide
lens of a telescope, everything is
smaller, condensed. Part of a country

which rules the world, you no longer
feel part of it. History, that is. Crossing
the Seine has ceased to console.
It is just a river. The waters stirred.

LOVERS AND SONS

1 *The Lover* by Marguerite Duras

You open a book, and an old woman speaks,
over her ravaged face, how a stranger
accosted her one day, told her he preferred

this present dissolution to her photo at
seventeen, gazing out from the Gallimard cover.
A French woman child, a Chinese lover—

Who knows where these obsessions start?
My father's lost sexual desires? My own wayward past?
The internment, surely the internment.

And how the world shrinks to this room, body, cry.
How the world shrinks. How the roads of French
Chochin China weren't invoked in Paris for years.

How I slept once with one who came from there,
almost a child-woman, and wondered why she,
unlike the child-woman in the book, did not

bleed, but cried out my name in a language
not her own, caught in history, and this lover,
who betrayed her and the white woman he loved . . .

2 Saigon, 1930

Afterwards, in a room of diaphanous volatility.
She's always known it would be like this,
dark lethargy and emptiness drifting inside her.

She strokes his body, the flesh so sumptuously
soft, as of a long convalescence, drained by fever.
And silken, without hair. Ambiguously shifting,

his features are aloof, unreadable,
like the sea of the tropics, the doldrums, a
gold opalescence shimmering to the horizon.

Touching her as always with a tentative calm
that masks his fervency; weak, helpless,
he knows his being will be eviscerated

if she ever ends this moaning and motion
of their bodies, this knowledge like nightmare,
so far from pleasure, but never desire.

Outside, the city crackles, a radio caught
between stations, shudders of white noise
and shadows through the blinds, a high-pitched

opaqueness upon which he rises, peers
through the cracks, lights a cigarette, lets the smoke
drift through the massive humidity and heat.

The air smells of roasted peanuts, burnt sugar
and soy sauce. Jasmine, incense, herbs, dust.
She thinks of the small village where she's grown,

far from the glittering capitals of her people,
lights, palaces of the Sun King, operas and art.
She's overwhelmed by nothing, this woman, this girl—

Not his English cigarettes nor his exquisite perfume,
nor the silk tussore that smells of liquor, smoke
and decaying fruit. He is like a hothouse flower,

much too ripe and rich. He doesn't call her
whore or slut, though she'll write it down
like that, years later. And yet, this is

how he thinks of her, her dirty white skin.
How he thinks of his own putrid, rounded face,
the face of a prig, or a million others like him,

all indistinguishable and unremarked. (That's why
all about them there's nothing, not even their bodies,
that cannot be taken, imprinted, owned, destroyed.)

3

Are there nights I dream of the camps,
my father roughhousing among boys bound
for the white dust of the ball diamond (and later Europe)?

Or am I guilty of—exploiting isn't quite the word—
am I responsible for a certain posturing and false purity,
an infantile predilection to see myself with the victims?

—I don't know. Each morning, I can't recall a thing.
What I know draws on these pages, this book:
That myself, the Chinese, my father are all bound

preposterously here, if only in these lovers
limning my psyche's depths and resemblances.
Oh, I was never the Chinese, never stood

in a restaurant unfolding before the white trash
of her family, my roll of bills, inviolable
amid the din of customers, the off tune

trumpet of the colonial jazz band, reveling
in their destitution and amazement at the money,
so much money I don't bother checking the bill.

I could not buy my hungers in such fashion.
And yet, I might have, had I that option,
had the child-woman appeared beside me

on the ferry, in a man's fedora, a loose
white dress, the gaudy heels of a prostitute.
And yet, scrying this screen of longings,

how deeply I've conscripted her consciousness,
how alien his, despite his race, is to mine,
perhaps I'm all wrong, my perspective skewed,

what I desire isn't to possess, but to be her—
knowing a white girl on this ferry's not only odd,
but a kind of performance? To be so ached for,

even by a Chinese, even as I protest to mother,
how could I, how could you think, with a Chinese,
when she accuses me in my room, rips my dress,

slaps my face, screams I'm a whore,
she's reared a whore, all the colony is talking?
Still, why wring such questions from the body

history has bequeathed me? Who the fuck
cares? you ask, and I would agree with you.
That's why I know the Chinese, why he exists

within me, why I want to shout when her brother
shoves his face against mine, dares me to
strike him, curse, push, provoke, do something.

"It would take two of you to beat me," he says.
And I, with my only smile of the evening, reply,
"It would take four. You have absolutely no idea how weak I am."

4

And later the girl, the woman, with a slight gesture,
hollows a haunt for herself on my chest, and as rain
shudders and gusts into the room, sets us shivering,

she cries she's going to be happy, I must be happy,
I must love the Chinese who will become my wife.
She says she'll never forget my scent; I reply

it's her child's body, its gaunt elongations
and boniness. Later, I tell her of the fabulous
house in Sadec, its blue terraces and lacquered

interiors, floors scrubbed by servants like penitents,
patiently shining the path of a god. Of course,
I cannot break from my father, arrangements

merging his wealth with the family across river.
It must all go according to plan. It must all go.
(Even now, the plans, like my clothes, my vices,

are gleaned in Paris, in libraries and cheap cafés,
in humiliations of an immigrant, a student, a dog
from the colonies, who has named himself Minh.)

She asks where my money comes from.
Gold, tea, porcelain, I reply. *Also opium.*
She knows nights she isn't with me, I sleep

in those dens, still as a drowned man, a penitent
whose mind has left him staring with vacant eyes,
which then close. She asks if she's like that for me,

in those dark cubicles, tucked inside their wombs.
The need. The ache. I lean back, stare at cracks
mapping the ceiling; riotous drops pock the roof;

drippings catch in huge clay jars in the corners.
I fold my hands on my chest. It's as if I were dead,
or listening to a concert, or my own heartbeat.

Jade too, I say. *Silk and jade.* On the Mekong,
junks moor at the banks, a cormorant shivers
on a log. A baby cries. And darkness creeps upriver,

into the forests, the immense forests of the uplands,
sources of this plain, vast alluvial deposits
where the soil commences and ends with the sea.

So my words mingle with hers, a meaning
created, lost with each sentence, regained only
when I'm on her, masquerading as conqueror,

evil at the gates, slicing sheaf after sheaf of skin.
What is this intoxicatingly foreign lullaby,
whose words I've memorized and can't understand?

Did my parents ever sing such a song? Why
seek where such tunes begin? Father, forgive me.
Marguerite, too. And her anonymous Chinese lover.

Phu, my student, Hoa, my lover, Tho, this servant,
the others of that colony. And she who reads this
and sleeps beside me. So much I owe you. So much left out. . . .

5 The Dream

And then, suddenly, in the dark night, the rain came.
The child was sleeping. In a voice that was vacant
and somehow filled with the shiftings of violence,

the Chinese, the Asian, said sadly,
"The monsoon has started." Then the child awoke
and became me, and softly listened to the Chinese

calling for the child to come, see the monsoon.
How beautiful and desirable the rain poured over
him and the child. And I knew it was my father

who desired me, not my brother or sisters,
and we would live in this house in the jungle
forever, and I could barely open my eyes yet

I started singing. So the child slept. The rain
stopped. The Chinese disappeared. I went on singing.
—What happened to my father? I don't know.

3

THE AFFAIR: I—His Version

As she slowly slid the silk scarf from her neck,
brushed it against my nipples, leaning herself
over me, hair like a waterfall, overflowing the
brim of desire, slotting it through the bedposts,
around my wrists, torso struggling, a field
of concentration beneath her, whipping
a rower's rhythm, I fell backwards beneath,
her image glaring like a sunspot before my eyes,
and the film stopped a moment, and I held it there,
the trauma, it was connected then to every other
moment of my life, it would not let go, like
filament after filament flung out to the dark,
catching somewhere, oh my soul . . . Who do
you think you are? Who let you in? Why are you here?
Oh I was a serious man devising complexions
of risk, canonizing what I knew to canonize,
drawing strength from whatever it was I was
whimpering over, cries unbraiding themselves,
loosening from a long strand that never seemed
to end, the infinite rope of desire and death,
witherings of human solitude. And always
she was reading this book, not one I wrote,
but interpretations, dreams and vexations,
curses, howls from the migrant wind, unsettled
but claiming everything about us. It was the truth,
she said. As I was her son, her boy. Golden,
brown, darker than exhaustion, cheeks smooth,
chest smooth, fingers delicate as slivers
of mown grass, as dry, brittle leaves, crackling
to the touch. She bent down, bit one off. Then
another. Sweet, fragrant. Tongue, lips tasting,

salt flourishings, brilliant blossoms. Feeling
her beside me, speaking, I was choking in silence,
and the smells of shoyu and chrysanthemums,
of grilled squid sifted about us, settling our skin,
faint and musky as her incessant whisper—
. . . And then there was only this room, and her voice
speaking, and the image of her feet at the bottom
of the bed, the nails beaten and gnarled, slate
colored like beach stones, and glimmering pubic hair,
wisps of blondness I would comb and comb
with my tongue, digging deeper in the furrow,
saying words I barely knew, outliving myself as prayer
and rain and the long slow descent towards despair.
In Tokyo or the Mekong. New York, St. Paul, Paris.
I was seeking abasement. I was seeking whiteness.
I was the native pouring myself into her light.
I was the jungle, compelling transmogrification.
Bright blossoms. Screeches. Comfort in a complicated house. . . .
And so, I was standing in grey light, thinking
this must be finished, forgetting how the rushes
of surf collect and re-collect grain after grain.
How I was bigger and emptier than anything
she could hold; how I ended it between us,
seeking this refuge, here . . . And still in memory
come the bodies ready to perform their bodily
music of forgetting this, this thing called whiteness,
consciousness, called you're leaving me all the same;
called I made you suffer too much, called I cry out
for a leg, a lip, a leveling of hip to hip,
wheeling us out of one hell into another, progenitor,
little biscuit of flesh to nibble in the night. Called
something taking its course here. Something in you . . .

❧

It's not so easy to start such things, the telling I mean,
not the deed. Let's try this: Did you ever enter anything
so vile, so revealing of your own darkness you can't
quite believe it ever occurred? Or found the course
of certain events in your life so clichéd and improbable
they might as well be mere fiction? Of course
you have. If you have reached anywhere near
a certain age, of course you have . . .
We met at this party. Instantly, I hated her, hated
her husband too, she in a black cocktail dress
and string of pearls, her eyes blue and furtive,
that I would catch gazing up at me as she bent down,
took a sip from her wine, while he stood beside her,
hand at her back, silver hair slicked back,
black jacket, shirt, pants, his face a craggy ruddiness,
the artsy version of say Jack Palance.
It was the way they talked about Tokyo, Paris, Berlin,
New York; the light Matisse loved in Morocco;
a restaurant they adored in Venice, her girlhood
on a Montana ranch, their words filtered through
the Gauloise they smoked and an assurance
resting so comfortably on the verge of caricature,
as if they knew they were protected not from criticism
or jealousy or spite, but from ever failing to
elicit in their listener an expected interest, captivation,
their singularity fused indelibly in memory.
For me it seemed more a class thing than race,
though at the time I was still trying to sort out the two.
I'd come to accept my presence in a room of whites
as completely natural, unremarkable as the presence
of delphinium or flight in your dreams. (No,
even more than that. It was, except for holidays with relatives,
all I experienced, all I knew.) And yet, not far from

the lintel of my awareness, there was no getting around
the fact that they were white, that what captivated and
enraged me were the compensations they were unaware of
in their beauty, in their so calmly entering the center
of my attention, in the correct proportion
of their presence together. And as each wave
of compulsion, comparison hit me, I hated them more,
filled with a *ressentiment* so textbook classic,
you would have thought it would have toppled me over
in my tracks, or even turned me around, walked me
straight back out the door to check the apartment
number, the address, the building, suddenly certain
I was in the wrong place. But of course I stood there,
listening, nodding politely; asking question after question.
And all the while, as she brushed her hair from
her face, as he slipped the cigarette from his mouth,
exhaling a white cloud; as my questions flowed
the conversation across continents, worlds beyond me—
I saw myself as a midwestern provincial, like Charles Bovary,
a bit oafish and subdued, using whatever slickness
I could muster from the garb of art as camouflage—

I wanted her. I wanted her.

❦

On a familiar ledge in my life I began to fashion
a language for desire, for the soft caving
inside me at the presence of sexual want,
for my own weakness and loathing and shame,
for the revenges I felt I needed against women,
their impenetrable otherness, their beauty, their
remoteness, and their skin, the whiteness of skin
spread before me like a map of the ramparts.
It was, I realize now, a type of madness, an ancient cruelty,
and the guises I slipped on in my assuming
seem so transparent now, though they
somehow did the trick. And it was a trick really,
those revanchist seductions, openings I sought for
in the other with the cloak of tenderness, concern,
a way of questioning which, as I remember,
seemed to say to them—I am the listener
you've always dreamed of, the one unencumbered
by the need to place myself, my story,
my observations and neuroses at the center,
the one who will provide you the attention and
basking you always desired in the affections of men . . .

In other words, reader beware. I was hardly
as innocent or naive as I may make myself seem.
Still, in this case, let me spare you
the cobra and mouse game of the chase, trying to
equivocate who was the cobra, who the mouse—
I was the mouse. And as I moved in there was this
constant hissing, this yes, no, yes, no, moving her words,
her legs, the way she bent down to pick up her glass,
a toss of her head, a smile. In the early stages
the obligatory homage to certain modernist giants
sifted through our conversations, mixed with gossip

about various artists we knew, or rather, she knew
and I had read about. From time to time, there'd be
a phrase she'd let drop, about her husband,
about being with me, though nothing had happened yet.
Of course, we were both aware something *was*
happening. Is it fair to say she knew more than me?
Certainly, this was a state of affairs I'd arranged
so many times before it inevitably brings to mind
the repetition compulsion. But what initial trauma
was I repeating? Where did it begin? Such threads
may unravel in so many directions, backwards
and forward, lingering in time. So what I offer now,
I offer as speculation, perhaps a theory that simply
puts a more human spin on my giving in to my baser,
self-destructive desires (I know such casual connections,
sociological and crude, can't possibly be substantiated):
Wasn't what I sought, suffered, desperately needed,
something more than merely personal, more than
the inevitable longings for the other, or if merely
such longings, couldn't they have been fashioned,
or imprinted, or self-concocted as some odd reenactment
of the fascination and seduction of my father,
of Japanese America, by the all white American dream
(I almost wrote "whore")? I mean not so much in the later years,
when Nisei after Nisei settled into a comfortable,
seemingly colorless bliss of suburbia; but in those years
just before and after the war, wasn't there this eagerness
inside my father, his generation, to be let in, this hypnotic
trance before the flag, patriotism, the Constitution,
that allowed them to wander, like ghosts, four years
in the desert, pursuing America's bright cheap promise.
But perhaps it's better to let go such specious musings:
For when I finally got her in bed, when she finally

lay beneath me, still beyond me, but not beyond my rage,
I know for certain I fucked her with all the fury
of a slave run amok, or Macbeth in the battlefield,
transmogrified to a face twisted like a demon, showing
how hard it is to be evil, punishing her being, her sins,
her whiteness adored. And of course, in an instant,
horrified, thrilled beyond belief, I saw it:

She loved it. She truly loved it.

Almost immediately it began to break down.
Or rather, she began to break me. Or rather, I asked her
by simply waiting, being there, lying there beside her,
as light slipped through the Venetian blinds, strips of brightness
across her body, as I shuttled my hand across,
and she began to talk, first dreamily, about nothing,
about the monumental heat of New York in July,
about that high mountain country where she learned to ride horses,
a vast plain rescued from savages; about Mardi Gras
in New Orleans, the silken delta, crawfish and jazz,
Faulkner's octoroons, and then it was her photographs,
at one stage swimmers, lovers, moving in fluorescent waters,
and later children, caught in poses where desires,
not quite raw or sexual, but sexual nevertheless,
seemed to seep in from under the surface, a ghost image
of adult seduction and want, provoking, revolting the critics
(they'd catapulted her, at least for now, to a plane in the pantheon).
Only occasionally would she talk about her husband;
he'd been writing this monumental novel for years,
fabulous in its rumors, his genius flourishing larger, bolder,
the longer it took. Only after months did I learn his family
                    connections,
vague allusions to a trust fund that kept them unfettered,
moving like gypsies; or how this movement suited her, connected
to the uprootings of her childhood, her father a stray hand,
moving from ranch to ranch, moving finally out of her life
(now she had no idea where he was, or if he were alive, it didn't
                    matter).
But the breaking, that was there from the beginning,
from when I first showed her my poems,
and she lay back against the headboard, smoking her Gauloise,
stubbing it in the ashtray, pausing in a long silence after she finished,
a slight sigh in her voice. And what she said, I realize now,

had this steady directness, though at the time it struck me
as some age-old gentility, some patrician air that came
not from her childhood or the worlds she'd escaped to since then,
but simply from the inherent superiority of being born the being
that she was, as if the survival and specialization of the species
had led to these moments of discernment, intelligence, a lucidity
that could only be mustered in leisure, exposures to a more luminous
       world.
She looked at me: "You don't really know that much yet, do you?
You're still groping. Oh, it's there, you have something,
but it hasn't surfaced. I'm not really talking about technique or
      education,
though those things matter. You can learn those. It's something else,
you're just too wrapped up. You're still trying to figure out
what's interesting and what's not. And what you think is
      interesting . . ."
The afternoons were unmoving, dense with heat, the washes of
      traffic.

I listened. I sat transfixed.

❧

Later, it became cruder. Unbelievably crude.
"No one wants to read about your minority background.
No one wants these little stories about Japanese people."
That was near the end, and, I see now,
from desperation, flinging razor after razor,
as if something might slit us open. As if she sensed
I too needed some abasement more blunt,
more penetrating, more raging to match the rage
and humiliation I felt before her, now that I loved her,
now that she'd infected my psyche, all the while knowing
how impossible that was. She, of course, never even bothered
to dangle it before me: "I'm not leaving Mark. You know that.
I've never lied to you." It was night when she told me this,
the sky cobalt, stretched over us like a tarp, mountains
like great ships moored about us, a wall of pines.
We were lying on the porch of a cabin, naked, sweating, chilled.
I pretended I was falling asleep. "It doesn't matter if you're not
            listening.
Sleep for all I care." She was telling me the story
of meeting Mark, how she left her first husband.
How she fled to Morocco trying to sort it all out.
One day she stumbled on this rug dealer who looked like Hendrix;
he drove her on his motorbike to a stone house outside the city.
They smoked hashish, and another man appeared. The men
started painting her with saffron, her face, her arms, legs,
until she started screaming, kicking, flinging the dirt floor in their
            faces.
"At that moment, I don't know why, I knew I would go with
            Mark."
She never knew why they let her go; she suspected they suspected
she would be too much trouble. "They were wrong.
If they had shot me with heroin, I would have made a great addict.
I would have never left. . . ." Suddenly

she got up, went inside, put on Mahler full blast,
the orchestra crashing like a wave over my body, up the mountain.
I yelled at her to turn it off. She pretended she didn't hear.
Later, after the tape ended, as I was really falling asleep, casually
she made this remark about my wife, I don't even remember what
       she said.
And that was it. I got dressed without a word, walked out the door,
and began walking down the road to Montpelier.
I never saw her again. Or spoke to her. Not that I still can't see her
       face.
Or hear her words. And for two, three years afterwards,
I hardly wrote at all. Squibbles. And I read everything I wrote
with that voice, that face, standing over the page, shaking her head—

"No, no, that's not it at all."

❧

None of this quite happened this way, just as the self I've written
          here
isn't quite the self who writes. There was never the one remark,
just as there was never that man at the grocery, insulting my father,
in that first poem of desire, though the memory of each burns
within me just the same. How I needed the aftermath. Her lack of
          praise.
At the end, it's not her I think about, but this image from mere
          fiction,
only with the narrative perspective reversed—Recall the native on
          the shore,
running with the current, glancing madly at Marlowe's steamer,
somewhere in the heart of his darkness, unaware still of how the
          puffing engine
and the pale ghostly face at the stern will send his gods up in vapor;
how soon one of his descendents will pore over some schoolbook,
find in configurations of natives and the masks of skin a mirror for a
          self;
how the student turns his gaze upwards to the master, who smiles
          back,
friendly for a moment, pulsing with certainties, self-knowledge,

a semblance like love.

THE AFFAIR: II—Her Version

You never know how long these things last, though at times you
        want them to go on
forever. It is like a quietness that descends, of rooms with immense
        ceilings, and marble
floors echoing footsteps. The light is northern, as up in the
        mountains, cerulean sky
and a sun shaft angled on our legs. A few beads of sweat, though it is
        late winter,
the caps on the lake frothed and curling, slapping stones. That is the
        sound we made,
the slapping of stones, of water on stones. I wanted it to stop, that
        instant, that instant
he entered me with the motions of cold fervency and desperation,
        the precision
of the abattoir. Or simply, a bedroom. Every bedroom that ever was.
        Every passion.

Sometimes I imagine I have a brother, who stumbles home from a
        night of dancing.
His hair is dark. Perhaps he's of a different father, a father who elicits
        from him
arias just as false as mine, but more fleeting. This is because my
        brother is a man
and even in his absence—for surely his father too left mother long
        ago—knows his father
as I know mother. And I do know her, her predictable silences and
        despair;
also something deeper, the blank emotions of those who watch and
        who are watched in turn,
the ungovernable, mute black rage that hollows her cheek like mine
        and makes her
in her beauty, uninhabitable, like the great stretches of the desert that
        astonish
with their sheer hostility to life. My brother, I suspect, knows
        nothing of her, me.
He is still in love with all women. His shirt drenched with sweat, his
        eyes bleared.
And though he's been drinking, though he's hobbled home alone, I
        can't tell if he holds
the same desperation inside. He's weaker than me. He's a man. He
        must keep trying.
He kisses me on the cheek, a little too close, asks me what I am
        reading. Leaves
before I can answer. I hear him whistling down the dark of the hall,
        and I can't
quite make out the tune, though I know his body has paid
        everything for it,
each fiber and muscle, bone, blood, as I have paid for mine. This
        singing I mean.

That man. He was writing about me the moment he entered the
       room, found me
repeating one of those speeches at one of those parties you can never
       leave;
as I glanced up from my wine glass, something slipped back in like a
       memory,
and the room was buoyant and familiar and utterly cold.
It was my brother. It was clear we would rent each other. Clear the
       entrails, quietly pulsing, would show.

❦

In my dream last night, I take him in my arms, the way you would a
           child,
cradling his head. He moans softly. Or I think I hear him moan.
He's afraid I'm abandoning him, like a baby pushed out on the river.
And the current flows past us, carrying the faces we wear this instant
           and the next.

All the incitements to desire are nothing to the witness we bring to
       our bodies.
My mother knew this, in the slips of insulting violence she let me
       see, the impulse to kill
or be killed she found in the last candid throes of her demeaning
       with man after man.
How she would turn so amiable, so trusting, when the next came
       along, keeping
herself quiet, finding miraculously some unused portion to trot out
       before him.
It was, for me, like watching a freak show. And so I left. Again and
       again.
And put myself beyond her, her men, the vague fragmented
       memories of my father
who suddenly returned one summer when I was ten, with two day's
       growth,
and this uncannily familiar liquor on his breath. And of course,
       mother took him in.
And ten days later threw him out. At sixteen, he came back again, in
       the morning
as I was leaving, my knapsack strapped to my back, about to set out
       hitching again.
We nodded at each other. Didn't say a word. I don't know what
       happened.
By the time I came back mother was selling her trailer, moving in
with this retired colonel she'd met in the lounge at the bowling alley.
I used to tell people my father was one of the first Green Berets
       killed in Vietnam.
(I liked to watch the look on their faces.) I don't know how I got
       from there
to here. I suppose the moment I stepped inside the bedroom of a
       man twenty years older.

And for a long time they were all like that, like my husband. Then,
      occasionally, younger.
But this poet, I'd never seen anyone so occupied with rancor and
      rawness, so much
wayward self-intoxication, all of it unformed, younger than any man
      I've ever been with
not in age, but as if he'd wandered in an instant as a spirit into his
      body, so alien
to his sensibility, he lived in terror of ever finding delight in it, his
      dark, rain softened skin.

What occurred between us remains an enigma. Think of the deserts
        where interrogations
and ablutions of the soul proceed into memory, chants, words on the
        page.
Or the way a woman might dilate her nostrils in amusement, seated
        at a long table
with dozens of other diners, each of them distinguished in their own
        way,
and she an attachment, like a bracelet or ring, or an afterthought, or
        thinking
of herself as an afterthought, which amounts to the same. Think
of a lacquered box of licorice, which a child raids in an empty house,
        all the servants
at their chores, oblivious to the theft. Or the sympathy you suddenly
        feel
for someone you have always despised, from the very first moment of
        meeting.
One day, in the near future, in some cabin, laying out my prints, I
        shall become
in an instant this incredibly old woman, my skin sagging as if to be
        shed.
Then, in the pilings and sea oiled stones abstracted in black and
        white before me,
brushing away the ashes of my cigarette that have fallen on the print,
his face, for a moment, will click into focus. And I will think of
        him. Like this. Like this.

❧

He had this habit of inserting his finger and vibrating it very rapidly.
It was sometimes pleasurable. Most often not.
I never told him either way. Either way it didn't matter.

He was, I am sure, constantly conscious of his beauty. Any
        declinations he makes
are the gaps obscured by his cold, implacable fascination with race.
        Color.
What he called the imperial age. But all this had nothing to do with
        him,
his absorption in himself, matching mine, demands we made on the
        mirror, so equal
only a vast gulf could have separated us enough to see the other,
        dreaming from end
to end, intermeshing our despairs. And whatever he might have said
        about class,
no one was more unsuited by temperament to empathize with those
        at the bottom.
Even if you stripped him, like Job, of wife, job, house, money, car,
        clothes, all
the material necessities of a being so thoroughly American of his
        time and means,
his doubts and denials that would sputter forth in frustration, in rage,
        even
in hopelessness, would be tinged with a certain airy smugness, an
        imperious assurance
he attributed to everything about me he could label whiteness,
        beauty, privilege.

❦

I saw him last month, by chance, at an opening. I did not panic, I
     said nothing.
And then, as if truly an apparition, I turned again to find only my
     own photograph,
a child running low to the ground, scooping pigeons in a park,
     flinging them
toward pleasures that come from flight, fear, the first sweet fervencies
     of power.

In the bath, he would wash my legs, urging frothy smears of suds
      back and forth.
I thought of a horse, exhausted after miles of hills, lathered and
      shuddering, the bit
still cold in its teeth. I think I was always running those hills, jawing
      the bit pulled tight.
And when I arrived at the stable, out of the darkness, he was there
      waiting, like a stableboy.
He smiled as he did this. And was enormously happy. "Your ankles
      are delicate,"
he said, "like a child's. But everywhere else. . . ." Unflinching was
      how he saw me.
And so what he worshipped was his own flight, nightmares roiled in
      humiliation
and scoured with ablations. I made no sound when he did this. And
      he smiled back.

❧

I thought his whole notion of genealogy so infantile, like his clinging
       to vague,
somewhat fascist notions of ethnic identity. God, think of the cobbles
       of Sarajevo,
and the rooms where the women are herded and overcome and left
       to their now
shameful, riven bodies. Or the wild searches afterwards for water, the
       ablutions
and thirsts that will not end. Or the trenches, spackled with limbs
       and oblivious faces,
staring up at spaces between the clouds. Or whatever opposing
       soldiers mutter
casually, with such force, over the handiwork of the day, so in love
       with cleansing,
with the purities they perceive in their own faces, in their hands and
       open mouths,
and whatever babbling nonsense with which they proceed to
       recognize their own.
He loved what was scandalous about us. That is what intrigues him,
       keeps him alive.
Not the present he constructs, hauling out the garbage of white
       trash, of which I am a part.

❦

We used to smoke a bit before. Once, it was hash, mainly grass. A
       ritual of sorts.
He liked undressing me slowly. Rarely was it quick or forceful,
       though it has been
with others and not without pleasure. I see us in a small white room,
       linen
curtains, a white chenille bedspread, stone tile floors, that flatten your
       feet with cold.
Cheap artificial flowers on the bedstand. The black hands of the
       clock, as I slip off
my watch, jerk towards the next moment, the next hour. His hands
       clamp my breasts
like an adolescent, a fascination with the layers of cloth beneath
       touch. We kiss.
A questioning, delicate tongue, then harder, more insistent. Beneath
       black silk pants
I feel him, he is small, delicate there too, this is who he is.
       Something larger
would be too gross for the clarity and coldness of his sensibility, great
       oceanic depths
where creatures writhe and thrive on the floor without sight. It was
       like that with him,
like searing through layer after layer of brine, without the need of
       breath. . . .

❦

Dissolved in his directions—"you are so wet"—or "louder, call out
        my name."
I felt silly and abandoned, interrupted. This was part of the chase
        scene. A pile up,
the metal careening and crumpling, the smell of spilled oil, a hiss of
        steam, no flames.
The roads we drove to arrive were twisted as a birthcord. Yet
        whatever drew us
was pushed with a tenderness. He was right in that. I am a great
        addict.

His hands move to my face, which he cradles, as if he believes in
    tenderness.
I know differently. I play along. How shall I say this? There is always
    this stiff
remoteness, even in his most fluid motions, as if he were looking at
    me
from the wrong end of a telescope, seemingly so far distant I am
    barely visible
beneath him, as he slips so decidedly, so dutifully downwards, nuzzling
cuneal hairs, the tongue re-creating those motions that have just left
    my mouth.
And then, then I know it will go on, and on, and I am to go on and
    on, and only
when he knows, in the grotesque and athletic convulsions that erupt
from the chakra of my body, flowing outwards, only when he knows
    the first
of my pleasures has broken—it's the sheen he's pressing himself to,
    that color
and salt fragrance and humus, glistening with interior smells, his own
    drug—
only when the opalescent moisture flowing there is already mine and
    his,
with my fingers gripping and guiding, almost inserted as an
    afterthought,
he enters me, expanded somehow beyond what I have gripped,
    enormous, unrecognizable
as body or face or man, but this presence I want to be rid of
    immediately after—
To be secure, possessed of solitude once more, washing him from me
    in a hot spray . . .

PIERCE COLLEGE LIBRARY
PUYALLUP WA 98374
LAKEWOOD WA 98498

—When I wake it is hours, he's breathing in my ear, and I turn
                away. The room
is black, cold, I can barely make out the shape of the dresser, the
                lamps, clothes
slipped over chairs like sheets of escape. I've been dreaming of a
                photo, one
that's afflicted me ever since I saw it. It's of a Chinese, being
                executed, saved,
said the caption, by order of the emperor from the ghastlier burning
                at the stake
for the Ten Thousand Cuts. And so, stripped by a surgeon without
                fanaticism or religion,
in precise layers and joints, the flesh is eased from the body, and the
                Chinese,
already limbless, perhaps flurried towards some other state by
                injections of opium,
or the body's virile, afflicted narcotic, or now without consciousness
                yet
with open eyes, he looks up towards heaven with a look a voice
                inside me
hesitates to name as ecstasy, though the suspicion arises nonetheless,
                and is,
like the photo, never quite banished from my consciousness. And so,
                in my dream
collage, working in my studio, all their faces are meshed, the
                Chinese, the crowd,
the Japanese, dozens of darker others, and in the tiny spaces between
                each body or face,
I paste sea anemone, various dark, smooth, oval stones. Who
                understands such things?
Sometimes at night I have these premonitions within my body, and I
                wonder

who it is will next take over, adulterating, misrepresenting me, inside
me tonight.

My husband, of course, had little to do with us. He has his own
      wanderings and obsessions,
engaged with his never-to-be completed masterpiece which has, like
      an assassin,
tracked him into middle age. An assassin who patiently waits for the
      moment in the study,
as the victim pores over pages, incessantly scratching out, replacing,
      emending,
fidgeting towards *le mot juste*. Suddenly the victim feels this pain, first
      in his arm,
then his chest, and he'll know what has happened, has always known
      it is coming.
My husband may even think I have sent him, the one who sneaks up
      from behind,
but were it me the blade would be larger, heavier, axing through the
      skull like butter,
cleaving those marvelous millions of cells spewing forth word after
      word between us.
The Japanese was never like that. Despite his airs, he was of this
      world. Even if now,
in his oblique attacks, in his clumsy ambition, he believes he is
      writing of us, scouring
for the clues that will lead him to his bounty, his trashy immortality.
      There was no "us."
That was mere illusion. Like the regions of the soul where sacredness
      takes hold.

🎋

There is a way a woman, whatever color, clings to the underbelly of
        privilege,
camouflaged as it were, by her positioning beneath, as if her less than
        powerful hungers
made her completely powerless and innocent. Betrayed, bereft,
        unaccountable.
Seeing that in myself I could see that in him, a current streaming
        beneath the surface
of our obsession with surface, the guileful beauty of the other that
        eludes us,
and so, in our jealousy, desire. It was this limbo we played at, who
        could twist lower,
debase their presence more. At the end, I think, I bowed before the
        master.
And he, in his bowing, never outdone, never noticed what had fallen
        between us.

❧

When I said no one wanted any more of his Japanese stories, this is
      what I meant:
That whatever abrasions suffered by him or those victims he claimed
      to speak for,
had to be imagined with a scrupulously neutral intent, impassioned
      perhaps,
but always alien, a stranger in a strange land speaking to strangers,
even if those strangers seemed to be one of your own. (And more so
      if truly strangers.)
This made him furious and unforgiving. Racked with unimpeachable
      righteousness
and doubt. And he never seemed to guess that in the annihilating
      angel he thought
he'd encountered, as out of some irrepressible nightmare, I'd only
      given him back
a part of himself he cherished and had elided and erased, so
      stubbornly eluding his art.

❧

"I know who this person is, this Japanese, this American, and you must
        never repeat this—
It started with nearly boiling sake, a kotatsu, a wet winter evening in Tokyo
when the dampness sears into your bones, and you can never get warm,
except for those few minutes emerged from the bath, breathing pores of steam.
We were interrogating Foucault, the Pathétique was on the stereo. It was one,
two o'clock. He lived nearby, there was no need to think of the last train.
But that was merely pretext, his staying meant nothing to me. My husband?
He was on sabbatical in America, not a novelist, but a linguist, excavating
        beneath sentences
archaeologies of meaning. I could have waited for him in Berlin (this was
        before the wall
cracked into fifty million pieces tearing towards the West). A Noh mask on
        the shelf
above us, one of those ethereal, unreadable beauties who later recoils to a
        wraith
so measured and predictable you might think its purpose to elicit the laughter
of pastiche, and never terror. I saw his hand fall, ashes tapped from my
        cigarette.
I had met other Americans but he was not like them, he was like no one at
        all.
I talked to him of Noh, the gentle charm of Canetti, reading Broch. I told
        him
once, through the hills that were Prussia, my mother rode horses. Now she
        dines out
and attends, with assiduous regularity, the opera and mass. I haven't seen
        her in years . . .

❧

"*In Japan, where I found myself was not where I thought I would be.*
And, in many ways, I am still looking for whatever it was I lost. It was
        never him, though,
and though I understand why, in the perambulations of his poses,
I was transposed in spirit, like the shifts of reincarnation, into another body,
all the while, the body that emanates so dark and aggressively from his lines,
despite her blondness, resembles me so little my inspiration seems utterly
        fantastical.
I could have never managed all that sturm und drang *despair. Odd that he*
        could be
so American and write so Germanically. (Or perhaps that's my own
        ethnocentrism?)
I remember when he left the last time, and you know, we never, never ever
        touched,
I caught this look on his face that was really quite remarkable, as if I'd
        deceived him.
After he had insulted me like that—"I don't want to have a petite
affaire.*"*
What was he talking about? And yet, in the glow of the balcony light from
        the dark
of my apartment, his face seemed opalescent, quiet and cold as the moon.
And in the last of this series of moon hills, I can sometimes see him, slanting
        out
from the shadows, then vanishing as quickly as he came. Perhaps in a small
        way
that evens things out a bit, after all he has written, sentence after sentence of
        lies."

THE AFFAIR: Coda

Think of the cold exhumed from pages of a book left on a sill on a
          winter night,
blowing from word after word as you leaf through, looking for the
          passage you suddenly recalled,
but cannot find. Say the window looks out on a lake in the
          mountains. In Italy.
And there's the steps and shouts of the last workmen, who have
          cudgeled
the cobbles all day below, leaving. The sound of lukewarm water
          filling the bath.
Aqua minerale on the bedstand. The armoire half open, revealing an
          array of dark dresses,
as of a widow in mourning. You pass over a description of red
          pantiles, lemon trees
dripping with mist, the footman with the umbrella, and the terrors of
          impeccable taste.
It is, you suddenly recall, the wrong book. And you place the book
          back on the sill.
These are rooms you have made love in. They are all being fused
          into a single scheme.
And the book, with its damask welter of luxury and vague
          misgivings, is one
you've read too many times to have forgotten. And yet you don't recall
          a word.

4

HARVEST AT MINIDOKA INTERNMENT CAMP

after a watercolor by Kenjiro Nomura, circa 1943

Fingering the crescent pea pods, their squeaky skin,
bending and rising, ripped from the vines, fingering,
becoming, in a line, a line of motion, all one and green,

and slicing through the far mountains, a cumulus stream,
sunlight washes over you, over us, *okaa-san, nee-san.*
And giggling children draw rings in dust by the barracks,

watch the women, mornings, when the peas are pearled
with dew, glistening as foreheads glisten towards noon,
kerchiefs binding brows, the harvest flicked to baskets,

their implements burnished with callus, hard and delicate
as diamonds, sharp as steel, fingers that wash an infant's smile.
Everything flows, fox gloves at field's edge, river beyond wires,

a line of bodies, like shadows of clouds, shifting down rows,
and the chorus they sang—". . . under the apple tree," "*sakura*"—
how can I know? (And all the while, I know mother knows.)

Minidoka, I recall only this woman I knew for years. Peas
she set steaming, tumbling before me, tiny indented pebbles
I pushed about. How I refused. Her voice measured, cold.

GARDENS WE HAVE LEFT

1

As Sam fingers lumps of tofu on her tray,
I sizzle onions in oil, *shoyu,* rice wine,
toss noodles, ginger, sugar, *shitake;*

shoots of bamboo and chrysanthemum leaves.
Before the beef, veined with fat, thin as gauze,
I stir what for years I could not love.

(As a child, I shunned *mochi, futomaki,*
loved hot dogs, baseball, the GI John Wayne.
Now my *hashi* hauls up steaming *sukiyaki.*)

Later I take Sam out back, dressed in her *happi,*
and hum to her a nursery ditty
on the devil digging tatties with his shovel.

Yanking drooping petunias, scattering petals
like a cyclone, she tramples through the garden.
Soon she's crumbling parsley, mint, basil,

vines blackened dry as ash; now she splatters
tomatoes, half-caved in, shriveling with rot.
If this were August, I'd shout and stop her,

but since it's autumn, the clouds burnished, cool,
I let it spill from her, some giggle caught
from you, how her spine stoops and curls

like yours as you weed, trowel or clip flowers.
The air darkens, milky galaxies pour over us.
As I pick her up, Sam points, "Star . . . star . . . star . . ."

Feeling her weight, I think how someone
someday will call her *gook,* as surely as
this taste of ginger breathing on my tongue;

how the other day at this wedding, you
were matron of honor, and the priest greeted
you: "Oh, I've heard so much about you.

You must have such a large heart, it's so
generous of you to adopt this child . . ."
Suddenly, I envision—why would I want to

see this?—a white sheet descending, mapping
the body of my father, his dark leathery face
almost blue, like a baby before the slap

that shuttles its howl out to the world.
The sheet washes him from sight, the way
surf sucks up footprints from the shore—

Who will tell our daughter about the dark
gardener's boy who swam the Venice surf,
who never returned to L.A. after the war?

A late moth, a few crickets. I hear you call
us, the skin on our bodies, warm at last.
A man holds his child, sees his father laid

out in the sleep of his death. The wind
brushes his face. And then, it's his child's hand.

2

Suppose I try to tell Sam of my grandfather,
his J-Town hotel, pool hall or nursery?
I know so little even of father's fatigue

at his dim-lit desk at INS, as he rested on
his typewriter, deadline approaching, the keys
leaving little circles of letters on his brow.

Neither he nor my mother talk of the past;
my childhood myths are Saturday's cartoons.
All my father recalls is a March marriage,

unfurling in a damp cold room, how the groom
believed in Shakespeare and the flag, in my mother
giggling amid a crowd of Nisei girls, the band

bopping out "Begin the Beguine." It was 1950,
after the camps, the war, all the West Coast hysteria
lost in yellowed headlines no one retrieved.

Yesterday, at the campus grill with my blond, blue-
eyed students, over burgers and fries, Gordon
Hirabayashi spoke of refusing the '42 curfew,

how he wandered all night the Seattle streets.
Finally, foot-weary, hackled, he slapped open
the Police Station doors, strode to the desk,

and ordered they arrest him in his civil protest.
For months he would pace his cell, roaches
like sparks scattering from his steps,

and after countless prayers to his Quaker God,
he stood before the Court and uttered a "no"
they refused to hear. Sent to camp without a ticket,

whistling in the dark, he thumbed his way there,
wild hares scattering across the white-lined asphalt,
the Dipper spilling overhead its cup of stars . . .

With wire-rimmed glasses and hair softly greying,
looking almost a double of my father,
he reached into that era, held it before me

pulsing like a vein. And I somehow knew:
Had *he* been my father, had my father spoke once
like this, I would not be dabbing *shoyu*

from the chin of our *happa*-eyed daughter;
your Pilgrim face could not have compelled me
in quite the same way. Love, did my desire

sprout where history died? It's all speculation.
We are together. My father is alive.

3

Of course, it's an old tune—people migrating
across a river, a mountain, an ocean;
embarking, disembarking, leaving luggage,

customs, finding homes, lovers, children . . .
Who cares about past gardens, relocations, or race?
You and Sam take a bath; I wash dishes.

And the Buddha dies nightly on the road.
Perhaps I've learned to say: This is my home,
this yard where squirrels forage pine cones,

popcorn and pumpkin seeds from our garbage,
where our daughter's fears are measured
in sparrows, shadows, the mongrel next door

banging his cage. Where nightly I prepare
neither for angels or some Virgil
but the bottle and teddy bear and lullaby books.

So why do I insist on telling you this tale?
In 1944, set free with a sharp jolt, like lightning
loosed from a cloud, my father stood

outside those gates in Jerome, waving
back at his mother and father, their faces
sectioned by wires, like pieces of

a puzzle or invisible windows. Dust
puffed up a ridge where a bus reared
into view, and the young man, impatient,

stepped out of memory and into a world
without obligations or magic, prosaic
as that campus in Kalamazoo, where he

would stroll beside white coeds and the young boys
like him, breathing in a fragrance of
burning leaves, perfume and war.

Soon the landscape darkens so early,
the last sun skimming Arkansas hills,
swamp rot and mist drifting where

bullfrogs and crickets unsettle the night,
and an owl houses in his sight something
scurrying below. In the barracks, beside

the beds, now empty (he is the next to
last child to leave), *otoo-san* and *okaa-san*
fall into each other's frail limbs, listen

to the rain plop through cracks in the roof,
the storm overhead marking their loss.
Three hundred miles away, their son

peers out the window, a cigarette
glowing before him in the dark. His face
looks lonelier than I have ever seen it.

And I see now he too is like a window
I have gazed through all my life. How
little I have gazed at him in wonder.

This too, like Sam, is my hymn to America.

4

There are years the earth devours. What is it father
says of the camps? "In L.A. each day I'd sweat
and shove a mower for my father

across the lawns in Beverly Hills. During the war,
after school, I played baseball." Hey, Buddhahead,
how do you link amnesia with desire?

At fourteen, after school in my room in Oak Park,
I traced fashion ads from papers, stripping
white models, sketching in nipples, pubic hair.

Why did I start that gallery of obscene despair?
Out of that garden where the serpent hisses,
years ago, my great-grandmother carved

daikon to the bulbous head of a penis,
paraded to the shrine with *daikon* members
held erect by the Shingu women, their clogs

wobbling through the mud: It was harvest,
in the fields fires burned stubble to ash.
And the mountain gods whispered through cedars.

And the women sang, and later roasted and ate
those members, their teeth crooked and black.
—Suppose I had loved a woman like that?

Would I still be singing to Sam of wishing stars,
the blackbird that flings its caw from the eaves,
of ghosts and fairies, of walking amid flowers

just above the underworld, its demon caves?
And will she know I lived there once, and sat
in dark booths where the images displayed

whiteness as paradise made flesh, a bar where
nothing expires but consciousness spliced
in x-rated loops: come cry, scotch, and shudder,

dope, poppers, bodies that fueled my racial rage?
(So often, standing at the door, mumbling casually,
"I'm going to the store," I'd watch you gaze

up from your studies, and for a second, sigh—
Hours later, I'd return, the lie still inside . . .)

5

So often I go back to a greenhouse of roses,
each thorn bearing a droplet, each droplet
a sphere where you could spy a rose

or a spy according to your skin. How does
that song end? After grandmother's death,
after returning to the rebuilt rubble of Tokyo,

grandfather was buried somewhere on Koya-san,
amid graves of samurai, presidents of *kaisha,*
carpenters, priests, merchants and courtesans.

Years later, when my aunt traveled to find his grave,
she searched for hours amid century old stones.
Near evening, on the moss-heavy path,

in the cedar shadows, she broke into tears
at ashes irrevocably gone. Is this our legacy?
The past lies in this vase. The vase disappears.

I will say it now: In that soft-silted carbon,
the burnt flecks of bone no Nikkei can find,
what's missing is a history, a man, a nation.

In the months after Pearl, as headlines declare
Nips on the coast nurture fifth columns,
cajoling Gen. Dewitt, his military nightmares,

is a JACL Nisei who knows no Japanese,
who swears by Saturday reels of Errol Flynn
shooting savages for God, flag and Gary Owen.

(This Moses foresees in the sands of Anzio,
in shrapnel some Nisei will bleed at the Bulge,
the pride of purple hearts, P.R., and heroes.)

At panel after panel, he *asks* the authorities
to isolate Issei (in private suggests they brand them);
proposes internment to prove our loyalty,

and proclaims in some senator's ear
how unfamiliar he is with Buddha, how Christ
and the flag have made his accent disappear.

And later, in the camps, as JACL'ers
finger No-No's, *Kibei* and other resisters,
and even suggest marrying out their sisters . . .

Suddenly I think of your face, our daughter's—
Where did I learn to love? Are these my fathers?

6

Who pardons fathers now and so long ago?
Or blesses my digging like a worm the gardens
of Shingu and Jerome and Little Tokyo?

Some Masaoka, some Hirabayashi,
some grandmother's daughter named Ruth,
who hated for years the sight of any Japanese;

the soldiers who left their breath and blood
foaming and swirling in the Anzio tide
or in dark stretches of some German wood,

or the ones who, like my uncle, returned
to signs proclaiming as before, "No Japs served,"
loud as the notices that kept them interned;

those that served and those who would not serve,
whose speeches are written out of the books,
some Frank Emi, a black belt grocer,

or Omura, the reporter, whose pages were turned
over to authorities for the higher good—
not one of them can yield those years again.

Why bring them to bear on this song, our daughter,
the vines she tramples and the fists of flowers
she sprinkles on the lawn? Though I'm her father,

I know how little can pass down to a child.
(You know how my father and I fought those years
I declared like a boy that I would not kill,

and had no quarrel with the slant-eyed Cong.
We did not speak of it for years. The years are gone.
And my father is a stranger. Who loves his son.)

Dear, although I've come now to thirty-nine,
and share with you this child who bears your nose,
my eyes, and what is neither yours nor mine,

all I can offer her are these rumors and stories,
this legacy halved or doubled as the case may be.

7

Tonight as you breathe beside me,
I think of how your body rolled beneath mine
moments ago, plunging over me

as I sank deeper, past the image of our daughter,
petunia in her fist, the aroma of sukiyaki,
Coltrane and love sounds a sirocco in our ears.

Perhaps something is endlessly tracing
inside me memories trapped and released
in the body, like the roses that replaced

daikon in my grandfather's soil, shot
with steam as the L.A. sun streamed through
a dozen greenhouse panes. How it should plot

in heaven I don't know; our garden is terrestrial,
owned by imagination, and in it our daughter
skitters up to my father, flings her arms at his knees

while behind him, in the shadow of a cedar,
as the temple bells echo into evening,
ojii-san, obaa-san clap their hands together,

and bow their heads . . . —Think of all
the devourings of flesh, the way a babe
suckles, nuzzling the nipple with gummy jaws,

or how some Mifune samurai slouches to his *hashi;*
how our daughter nibbles pea pods, grasses, beans,
or the earth swallows our dead, sanding

flesh, leaves, bones; peeling hair, eyelids,
bark, bugs and bacteria searing through soil.
What do I find here in the gaze of a toddler,

this ancestral food, the lines my father once cast
in the L.A. surf, or those I paste to this page?
When you hold a great sorrow, it lasts

almost too long. And then it lasts some more.
But the same is true also of a great joy.
In the island of light we make with our bodies,

in the lullabies where our daughter sleeps,
we open a picture book, and the images are
for the first time. Once I lost something

of great value. And then I sought it.
Everything changed then. Everything changed.

IN AMERICA

The season of searing Santa Anas,
brush fires that flare all night in the hills, taut
vibrant emanations of light, *ojii-san*

would drive them to the Pacific, just before
sundown and the long steaming L.A. night.
In that silver Packard reeking of cigar,

the children laughed and shouted, sang with him,
never understanding the words, China
nights, a soldier somewhere in Asia, swimming

in his solitude, the girl from home. Soon
he shuttled them out beneath the night sky,
and he talked on the beach of his boyhood

in Shingu, his father, going back to Japan
for *omiyai,* their mother. Told them again
they'd been born here, this was their homeland,

but someday he'd go back to die, rich as an emperor.
Nonsense, says his wife, as they clamber back,
and he opens the door like a chauffeur,

tipping his cap. The children giggle. And none
of them knows this life is condemned,
even as they fall asleep to his humming,

syllables that flash and vanish in their dreams
years later in Chicago, Stamford, Miami,
cities of their small diaspora. They wake, groping,

to find the song vanished, a faint wind searing
their faces, still scented with sea, cigar smoke,
this sadness they cannot name. And each hears

only the breathing of a companion, blue
shadows of morning betraying a normalcy
none of them imagines, sleeping in the back

of a Packard in 1930, '36 or '40.
These are the years of expectation, elation,
when he is unbroken, she not yet dreaming,

as in the fall of '41, of flames soaring,
exploding off the sea, some divine wind
raining damnation, disintegration, war.

Years in America when my father was a boy.
When my father was a Jap. In America.

LISTENING

—for Samantha

And from that village, steaming with mist, riddled with rain,
from the fishermen in the bay hauling up nets of silver flecks;
from the droning of the Buddhist priest in the morning,

incense thickening his voice, a bit other-worldly, almost sickly;
from the oysters ripped from the sea bottom by half-naked women,
their skin darker than the bark in the woods, their lungs

as endless as some cave where a demon dwells
(soon their harvest will be split open by a blade, moist
meaty flesh, drenched in the smell of sea bracken, the tidal winds);

from the *torii* half way up the mountain
and the steps to the temple where the gong shimmers
with echoes of bright metallic sound;

from the waterfall streaming, hovering in the eye, and in illusion,
rising; from the cedars that have nothing to do with time;
from the small mud-cramped streets of rice shops and fish mongers;

from the pebbles on the riverbed, the aquamarine stream
floating pine-trunks, felled upstream
by men with *hachimaki* tied round their forehead

and grunts of *yoisho* I remember from my father in childhood;
from this mythical land of the empty sign and a thousand-thousand
              manners,
on the tip of this peninsula, far from Kyoto, the Shogun's palace,

in a house of *shoji* and clean cut pine, crawling onto a straw futon,
one of my ancestors laid his head as I do now on a woman's belly
and felt an imperceptible bump like the bow of a boat hitting a swell

and wondered how anything so tiny could cause such rocking unbroken
joy.

GLOSSARY

aka-chan—baby
furoshiki—scarf used to carry things in
gohan—rice
hachimaki—headband
hakujin—white person
happi—a short coat
hashi—chopsticks
hayaku—hurry
Issei—first-generation Japanese American
kaisha—company
Kibei—second-generation Japanese American educated in Japan
kotatsu—an electric heater
mochi—rice cakes
Nikkei—refers to Japanese who settle in another country
Nisei—second-generation Japanese American
obaa-san—grandmother
ofuro—bath
ojii-san—grandfather
okaa-san—mother
oshoshiki—funeral
otoo-san—father
sakura—cherry blossom (there is a famous Japanese lullaby of the same name)
Sansei—third-generation Japanese American
shoji—sliding door
shoyu—soy sauce
torii—Shinto gate
yoisho—heave-ho

David Mura's first book of poetry, *After We Lost Our Way* (E. P. Dutton, 1989), was selected by Gerald Stern as a winner of the National Poetry Series Contest. He is also the author of *Turning Japanese: Memoirs of a Sansei* (Atlantic Monthly Press, 1991), which has won the Oakland PEN Josephine Miles Book Award, and *A Male Grief: Notes on Pornography and Addiction* (Milkweed Editions, 1987).

Using poetry, creative nonfiction, and drama pieces, Mura has written and performed two multimedia performance pieces, *Relocations: Images from a Sansei,* and *The Colors of Desire* (with writer Alexs Pate).

Mura has received the US/Japan Creative Artist Fellowship, NEA Literature Fellowships, Bush Foundation Fellowships, a McKnight Playwright's Center Advancement Grant, a Loft-McKnight Award of Distinction, Minnesota State Arts Board grants, and a Discovery/*The Nation* Award. He has taught at the University of Minnesota, the Loft, St. Olaf College, and the University of Oregon. He is the artistic director of the Asian American Renaissance. He lives in Minneapolis, with his wife, Susan Sencer, and their children, Samantha and Nikko.